AUSTRALIA AND NEW ZEALAND

Australia and New Zealand are a very long way from anywhere, but that does not stop people from wanting to go there. To the Aborigines and Māori, these two countries were new homes that they could make their own. To the British, they were a place to put prisoners, and a land that could grow food for the hungry people of Britain. And today people go there from Asia, Europe, and almost every country in the world, to live there or just to visit.

And the most unusual things are waiting there. Farms as big as the country of England, and the steepest street in the world – it is hard to walk up it, and even harder to walk down! The biggest rock in the world, and a city where everyone has a holiday once a year – for a horse race. An animal with three eyes, and eleven men who do not play rugby until they have done a very frightening dance. If you are ready for surprises, come and see what life is like 'down under'.

OXFORD BOOKWORMS LIBRARY
Factfiles

Australia and New Zealand

Stage 3 (1000 headwords)

Factfiles Series Editor: Christine Lindop

CHRISTINE LINDOP

Australia
and
New Zealand

OXFORD UNIVERSITY PRESS

OXFORD
UNIVERSITY PRESS

Great Clarendon Street, Oxford OX2 6DP

Oxford University Press is a department of the University of Oxford.
It furthers the University's objective of excellence in research, scholarship,
and education by publishing worldwide in

Oxford New York

Auckland Cape Town Dar es Salaam Hong Kong Karachi
Kuala Lumpur Madrid Melbourne Mexico City Nairobi
New Delhi Shanghai Taipei Toronto

With offices in

Argentina Austria Brazil Chile Czech Republic France Greece
Guatemala Hungary Italy Japan Poland Portugal Singapore
South Korea Switzerland Thailand Turkey Ukraine Vietnam

OXFORD and OXFORD ENGLISH are registered trade marks of
Oxford University Press in the UK and in certain other countries

© Oxford University Press 2008

The moral rights of the author have been asserted
Database right Oxford University Press (maker)

First published 2008

4 6 8 10 9 7 5

ISBN: 978 0 19 423390 3

A complete recording of this Bookworms edition of *Australia and
New Zealand* is available on audio CD. ISBN 978 0 19 423589 1

Printed in Hong Kong

Word count (main text): 10270

For more information on the Oxford Bookworms Library,
visit www.oup.com/bookworms

Illustrations pp 2, 22 by Gareth Riddiford

The publishers would like to thank the following for permission to reproduce images:

Action Plus p 43 (Steve Bardens); Alamy Images pp 8 (John Daniels), 9 (Glen Allison), 10 (Worldwide
Picture Library), 11 (LOOK Die Bildagentur der Fotografen GmbH), 13 (Jon Arnold Images), 19
(Patrick Ward), 25 (Jon Arnold Images), 27 (Stillfx), 37 (Paul Grogan), 38 (Cupra Images), 40
(photomadnz), 53 (gkphotography), 54 (TongRo Image Stock); Heather Angel/Biofotos p 46;
Axiom Photographic Agency p56 (Rob Penn); Corbis pp 3 (Michele Falzone/JAI), 5 (Hulton-Deutsch
Collection), 31 (Robert Dowling), 33 (Frans Lanting), 35 (Paul A. Souders), 41 (Paul Almasy), 49
(Reuters); Mary Evans p 48; FLPA p 45 (Shin Yoshino/Minden Pictures); Getty Images pp 18 (Simon
Wilkinson/Iconica), 20 (Robert Frerck/Stone); Lonely Planet Images pp 17 (Manfred Gottschalk),
24 (David Wall), 42 (Jeff Yates); National Geographic Image Collection p (Jason Edwards); NHPA p
47 (Pete Atkinson); OUP pp 60 (barbecue/image100), 60 (sailing boats/), 60 (geyser/Corbis/Digital
Stock), 60 (kangaroo/Photodisc), 60 (glacier/Photodisc), 60 (koalas/Corel); PA Photos pp 51 (AP),
52 (ABACA Press); Panos Pictures p 15 (Penny Tweedie); Photolibrary p 34 (Robert Harding Picture
Library Ltd); Pictures Colour Library Ltd p 7 (Photononstop); Robert Harding Picture Library p 29
(Travel Library).

CONTENTS

1　An enormous land

What kind of country is Australia? Firstly, Australia is big – 7,686,848 square kilometres. In fact, only five countries in the world – Russia, Canada, the United States, China, and Brazil – are larger than Australia. One part of Australia, Western Australia, is four times as big as Texas, or eleven times as big as Great Britain. The journey from Perth in the west to Sydney in the east takes about four hours by plane; that is longer than the journey from Madrid to Moscow. And if you walk all around Australia along the coast, you will travel 25,760 kilometres.

Australia is also low and flat; only 5 per cent of the land is above 600 metres. But there are mountains in south-east Australia and in Tasmania. The highest mountain is Mount Kosciuszko, at 2,228 metres. It is in the Great Dividing Range, near the eastern coast.

Australia is hot and dry too. Two-thirds of the country, mostly in the centre and the west, is desert. There are hills and big dry salt lakes, and it is very difficult to grow anything. The temperature is often 35 °C or more in the summer months, and not many people live there.

There are some big rivers, like the Murray-Darling, which is 2,700 kilometres long, but in parts of Australia it sometimes does not rain for years, and 80 per cent of the country gets less than 600 millimetres of rain a year.

In the north, half of the year is 'wet', and half is 'dry'. From November to April heavy rain fills the rivers and makes enormous lakes where thousands of birds come for the

Indian Ocean

Pacific Ocean

Great Barrier Reef

Australia

Darwin

Western Australia

Northern Territory

Bungle Bungle Range

Alice Springs

Uluru

Queensland

Brisbane

South Australia

Cooper Pedy

Lake Eyre

Darling River

New South Wales

Sydney

Canberra

Australian Capital Territory

Mt. Kosciuszko

Murray River

Adelaide

Victoria

Melbourne

Perth

Tasmania

Hobart

0 km 300 600 900 km

N

summer. From May to October the north is often sunny and dry for weeks, and it is a popular place for winter holidays in the sun. *Winter* holidays? On this side of the world, of course, the seasons are different from the seasons in northern countries; December is in the summer, and June is in the winter.

Tasmania is cooler and wetter than the rest of Australia, with high mountains, thick forests, and some of the world's oldest trees.

So although it is true that much of Australia is flat and dry, it also has hills and mountains, rainforests, deep river valleys, and wonderful beaches.

In all of this enormous country there are only 20 million people. Most of them live close to the coast in the east, south-east and south of the country, where the summers are warm and the winters not too cold. There are only 2.6 people to every square kilometre in Australia – one of the lowest numbers in the world. (In Singapore, for example, there are 6,208 people to every square kilometre.) In fact, this means that there are large parts of the country with very few people at all. And 84 per cent of the people in Australia live on just 1 per cent of the land!

A forest in Tasmania

2 Australia's past

The first people in Australia were the Aborigines, who came more than 40,000 years ago from South East Asia. Chinese sailors visited 2,500 years ago, and much later Dutch sailors came – Willem Janszoon in 1606, and Abel Tasman in 1642. The Dutch made maps of the north and west coasts of Australia, but they did not try to live there. Then in 1770 the British sailor Captain James Cook landed on the east coast, and said that Australia now belonged to Britain. Nobody asked the Aborigines about this, and it was the beginning of a terrible time for them.

Until the 1780s Britain had sent convicts to the United States when it had too many of them for its prisons. After the Americans won the War of Independence in 1783, the British had to find a new answer to this problem – and the answer was Australia. In May 1787, eleven ships sailed from Portsmouth in England carrying 772 convicts. They reached Port Jackson – now Sydney – on 26 January 1788. Life was very difficult, and the convicts had to work very hard, making roads, buildings, and farms. In 1803, convicts were sent to Tasmania too. A few years later, people began to come from Britain because they chose to make a new life in Australia, and they went to live in South Australia, Victoria and Queensland as well as New South Wales.

In 1851 gold was found in New South Wales and Victoria. Thousands of people went looking for gold – first Australians, then people from North America, Britain, Ireland, New Zealand, and China. In ten years the population grew from

Looking for gold in the nineteenth century

400,000 to 1,200,000. With the gold came new roads and railways and growing cities.

On 1 January 1901 the six Australian states – New South Wales, Victoria, South Australia, Queensland, Western Australia, and Tasmania – became one country. Britain was still very important to Australia; many people left Britain for a new life in Australia, but they still called Britain 'home'.

During the First World War (1914–1918) thousands of Australian soldiers went to fight for Britain in Europe, and more than 60,000 of them died. In the Second World War (1939–1945) Australians fought in Europe and Asia, first helping Britain and then the United States.

After 1945 the Australian government realized that Australia needed more people, and they opened the country to immigrants. People still came from Britain, but others came from countries like Italy, Greece, Germany, the Netherlands, Turkey, and the Lebanon. Since 1945 more than 6.5 million people have moved there, and recently people from countries like Vietnam and Cambodia have moved there too.

3 Eight cities and the outback

In each of Australia's six states – New South Wales, Victoria, Queensland, South Australia, Western Australia, and Tasmania – there is a large city which is near a river and near the sea. More than half of all Australians live in these six cities – and many others live near to them. In fact, most people live only a few kilometres from the sea.

Sydney, in New South Wales, is the oldest and biggest city, with 4.2 million people. It is built around an enormous harbour – some say that it is the biggest natural harbour in the world. It is a busy modern city and its tall buildings are the centre for a lot of Australian business. It is also an international city where you can eat food from all over the world, or just visit some of the thirty wonderful beaches!

When they think of Sydney, many people think of the Sydney Opera House. The roof of this beautiful building looks like sails on Sydney Harbour. It was opened in 1973 for music, theatre, and dance. Near the Opera House is one of the longest bridges in the world – Sydney Harbour Bridge.

Melbourne, in the state of Victoria, is the second biggest city, with 3.7 million people, and it was the capital of Australia from 1901 to 1927. In the 1880s people built many fine buildings in this rich city, and many of them are still there today. It has wide streets, some lovely old buildings, and many large parks and gardens. Like Sydney, it is home to

Sydney Harbour Bridge and the Opera House

many immigrants, and it has a large Chinatown. Melbourne's theatres and pubs are famous, and it is a popular centre for art, music, and festivals of many kinds.

Brisbane is in Queensland, on the east coast. Here the temperature can get very hot, and you can still find stilt houses – wooden houses on tall posts which let cool air under the house. Brisbane is an important centre for business, and many tourists also come to visit the city on their way to the beaches of Queensland or the Great Barrier Reef.

Adelaide in South Australia is called the City of Churches, and it is also famous for its city plan, which put parks all round the city centre. It has famous festivals of music, theatre, and film, and the WOMADelaide festival of world music and dance. From Adelaide many visitors travel to the Barossa Valley, where German immigrants began making wine in the nineteenth century. Some of Australia's best wine comes from here today.

A stilt house in Brisbane

Perth is a long way from the other cities, in Western Australia by the Indian Ocean. The land in the west has plenty of gold, oil, and valuable minerals, so Perth is a rich city. About one-third of the families in Perth own a boat, and swimming and sailing are part of life for nearly everybody.

Hobart in Tasmania is a smaller, quieter city, with a busy harbour, from which boats sail to the French and Australian scientific stations in Antarctica. The city began in 1803 with 433 people – 280 of them convicts. Now it has a population of about 190,000. Visitors to Hobart often go on to see Port Arthur, where the first convicts lived.

Finally there are two more cities – Darwin and Canberra – that are in territories, not states. (The Australian government has more power over what happens in the territories than in the states.) Darwin, in the Northern Territory, has no tall buildings, only long low ones, because during the summer storms the winds are sometimes very strong. In 1974 a storm called Cyclone Tracy killed sixty-seven people and destroyed nearly all the buildings in Darwin. Many Aborigines and immigrants from Asia live in the city, and there is a big army base here as well.

Canberra is in the Australian Capital Territory. Like many countries (for example, Brazil and the United States) Australia has a special part of the country which is just for its capital city. Canberra is the newest of the Australian cities, and its name is an Aboriginal word meaning 'meeting place'. It is also different from the other cities because it is a long way – 120 kilometres – from the sea, although it is on a river, the Molonglo. It was designed by an American, Walter Burley Griffin, in 1912, and became the capital of Australia in 1927. This beautiful city has thousands of trees, and a big lake in its centre. Canberra is the home of many important national buildings like Parliament House. The Australian government meets here, and many of the people in Canberra work for the government.

If you leave the cities and go to the flat, hot centre of Australia, you will find yourself in the 'outback'. The outback is more than two-thirds of Australia, but its population is less than 100,000. Many people live on sheep or cattle

Parliament House in Canberra

An outback road train

stations, which are enormous farms; there are a few cattle stations in Australia which are each as large as the country of England. The nearest neighbour is perhaps a hundred kilometres away, the nearest city 1,500 kilometres away.

People travel by road or by air. On the roads you can often see 'road trains', carrying cattle from the cattle stations. Small aeroplanes are used to take people, food, post, and machines to places that are far away from the towns.

Aeroplanes are also necessary for the Flying Doctors. At special times each day, people in the outback can speak to a doctor by radio and get help. Each station or house keeps a box of medicine, so that the doctor can say, for example, 'Take two of medicine Number 6.' If things are more serious, a plane will bring a sick person to hospital, or take a doctor to see them. Planes in the Flying Doctor service fly about 45,000 kilometres every day.

Children in the outback use the Schools of the Air. When these began, teachers spoke to the children by radio, and sent them their work by post. Now they use the Internet to stay in touch with each other and with their teachers. Once a year all the children spend a week together; the younger children go to Alice Springs, and the older children go to a big city, like Sydney or Adelaide. This gives them the chance to spend time with children of their own age.

Alice Springs is the largest outback town, with a population of 26,500. For about a hundred years it was just a small group of houses and shops, but recently the population has grown because it has become an important tourist centre. You can travel here by train from Adelaide or Darwin, and many tourists come to Alice Springs on their way to Uluru, the great rock in the desert.

The first white people who came to the outback used camels to carry themselves and their luggage. Now there are wild camels living in the desert, and there are farms with camels for tourists who want to try a journey by camel into the outback.

With radio, television, the Internet and aeroplanes, people in the outback feel less lonely than they used to. But the outback is still a hard place to live. From time to time tourists die when they drive into the outback without enough water to drink.

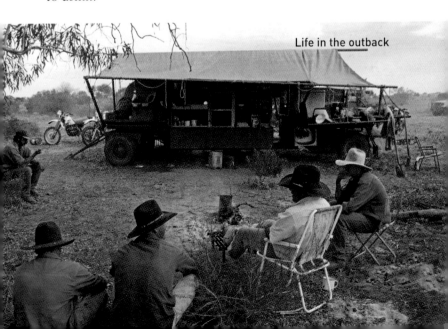

Life in the outback

4   The Aborigines

When British people came to Australia in 1788, they gave the name 'Aborigine' to the people they found there. The 300,000 Aborigines who lived in Australia at that time belonged to more than 300 different groups and each group had its own land and language. They travelled to different parts of their land during the year to find food and water; they ate plants and fruits and caught animals and fish. They did not own many things, and their only buildings were houses made from branches and leaves. This way of life did not damage or destroy the land where they lived.

At special times Aborigines came together in big groups. They painted their bodies and sang, danced, and made music. They believed that a long time ago the world was made by animals, plants, and humans together. This time was called 'Dreamtime', and there are many songs, stories, and pictures about it.

After 1788 their way of life suddenly began to change. The new Australians thought that because the Aborigines moved from place to place, the land was not important to them, so they took a lot of Aboriginal land and water. In fact, the land was at the centre of Aboriginal life. Thousands of Aborigines died in fights with the British or from the diseases that they brought to Australia. What happened in Tasmania is a terrible example. In 1804 there were between 4,000 and 6,000 Aborigines there. In 1831 there were 190. By 1876 there were none.

Between 1900 and 1930 special places were made where

An Aboriginal artist

the Aborigines had to live, far away from other Australians. There were now between 50,000 and 90,000 Aborigines living in Australia, and life was very difficult for them. They could not own land, they could not get jobs very easily, and their children could not go to school with white children. Nobody counted the Aborigines in the Australian population. Some people thought that there was no hope for the Aboriginal people, and many of their languages disappeared.

In fact, after about 1940 the number of Aborigines began to grow again, and now there are about 460,000 in Australia (about 2.4 per cent of the population). In some ways life is better; for example, some of the land that the British took now belongs to the Aborigines again. By 2002, the Aborigines owned 14 per cent of Australian land.

But for lots of Aborigines life is still difficult. Most now live in cities and towns, away from the land; the state with the largest number of Aborigines, for example, is not an outback state like Northern Territory or Western Australia, it is New South Wales. Although some have been successful, many feel that they belong neither to Aboriginal Australia nor to white Australia. Aborigines have more health problems and shorter lives (about seventeen years shorter) than white Australians. They leave school earlier, and it is harder for them to get jobs. Many of them find their way to prison – about 20 per cent of the people in Australian prisons are Aborigines – and they often have serious problems with alcohol.

In recent years people have begun to talk about another part of Australia's history. Between about 1900 and 1969, many children – perhaps as many as 100,000 – were taken away from their parents. Usually they were children with an Aboriginal mother and a white father. They went to live in

Aboriginal children

schools or with new parents, away from their homes and their own way of life. Many of them never saw their families again, and some did not even know that they were part Aboriginal.

In the late 1980s people began to talk about this. In 1998 the first National Sorry Day was held in Australia, to say sorry to the children who were taken away. Not all Australians agree about what happened, but they do now know about this dark time in Australia's past. The film *Rabbit-Proof Fence* (2002) made a lot of Australians think about the problems of Aborigines in the past and in the present. You can read this story in *Rabbit-Proof Fence* (Oxford Bookworms Stage 3).

At last now in some cities Aborigines are helping each other to learn about the Aboriginal way of life; young people are taken to the country, where older Aborigines teach them the songs, dances, and way of living of the Aborigines of the past. And perhaps more white Australians are beginning to realize that they can learn a lot about their country from the Aborigines.

5 Uluru and other wonders

One of the most beautiful things you can see in Australia is Uluru, also called Ayers Rock. It is an enormous rock alone in the middle of the desert south-west of Alice Springs. It is 3 kilometres long and 348 metres high, but there are another 2,100 metres under the ground. Uluru is 600 million years old, and for a long time people thought that it was the largest rock of its kind in the world. (In fact, Mount Augustus in Western Australia is two and a half times as big as Uluru.) Thousands of tourists come each year to walk round it and look at it. The best time to see it is at the end of the day, when its colour changes from yellow to gold, red and then purple. Some visitors like to see Uluru from a plane; others ride out into the desert to see it from a long way away. Uluru is a special place for Aborigines, and it belongs to the Anangu, Aboriginal people of the Pitjantjatjara group.

Then there is the Great Barrier Reef. At 2,500 kilometres it is the world's longest coral reef. Parts of the reef are 20,000 years old, and 1,500 different kinds of fish live there. It is very popular with tourists, who come to visit the islands and beaches, swim in the clear warm water, and take boat rides to see the fish and the coral.

Coober Pedy, which is about 846 kilometres north-west of Adelaide, is a really extraordinary place. The beautiful blue-green stones called opals were first found here in 1915, and more than 90 per cent of the world's opals come from here.

But it is very hot and dry – 35 to 45 °C day after day in the summer. So most people live under the ground in houses which are dug out of the rock. Here they can stay cool, and if they want a bigger house, they just dig another room! Coober Pedy's first tree was made of metal, and you can still see it on a hill outside the town. The Aboriginal name 'Coober Pedy' actually means 'white man in a hole'.

Lakes are usually cool and wet – but not in Australia. The big lakes of the desert are dry most of the time. Enormous Lake Eyre, which is 210 kilometres long and 65 kilometres wide, was dry for a hundred years until 1950, and the lake is only full of water about once every eight years. But now there is a Lake Eyre Yacht Club. When it rains, people who belong to the yacht club go to the lake to sail – while they can! Lake Mungo in New South Wales has had no water for 16,000 years.

Uluru

The Bungle Bungle Range

Another interesting place to visit is the Bungle Bungle Range in the Purnululu National Park in Western Australia. Here there are strange orange and black hills, made into round shapes by the wind and rain. There are also many kinds of birds and animals here, and Aboriginal paintings.

In Tasmania, 43 per cent of the land is covered in forest, and some of the tallest trees in the world are here. Some of the oldest trees are here too; Huon pines can grow for 3,000 years or more. There are seventeen different parks, with beautiful beaches, lakes, and rivers, and there are hundreds of different walks that you can take, from a few hours to several days long.

Finally there is the Todd River Regatta, a festival of boat races which happens every year on the Todd River in Alice Springs. The river is nearly always dry, so special boats are built for the races. These boats have sides but no bottom; the 'sailors' stand inside them and carry the boats as they run along the dry river bed. There are races for boats with two people, and races for big boats with ten people. The races end with a big water fight. Hundreds of people come to see these crazy races and enjoy the day.

The Todd River Regatta

6 Sheep, cattle, minerals, and wheat

Australia is a rich country, and life there is good for most people. Where does its money come from? Sheep, cattle, minerals, wheat, fruit, and wine are some of the answers.

Sheep have been important since the end of the eighteenth century. Most Australian sheep are Spanish merinos, which were first brought there in 1797. Merinos are strong animals and live happily in warm dry places. Now 20 per cent of the world's sheep live in Australia, mainly in New South Wales and Victoria, and 25 per cent of the world's wool comes from there.

Picking apples in Australia

Cattle are found mostly in the drier parts of the north and centre, and cattle stations cover one quarter of Australia. The meat from Australian cattle is sold to countries all over the world.

Gold made Australia rich in the nineteenth century. Since then, silver, other minerals, and oil from the Northern Territory, New South Wales, and Western Australia have made millions of dollars for Australia. But not everyone is happy about this. Digging for minerals often destroys the land, and there can also be problems when minerals are found on Aboriginal land.

Western Australia and New South Wales grow a lot of wheat, which is sold to the USA, China, and Japan. Australia grows other kinds of food, too. In Queensland they grow bananas; further south, where it is less hot, apples are grown. And in recent years, Australia has been making very good wine too. Australian wine is sold to more than ninety

countries, and the most important markets are the USA, Britain, Canada, and Germany. Australia also sells fish, sugar, and wood to other countries. When you look at everything that Australia sells, the largest part goes to Japan, followed by China, South Korea, and the USA.

But these days Australia is like many other rich countries, because now most of its workers do not work in factories or on farms. Two-thirds of them work in shops, offices, banks, or schools, and nearly 70 per cent of Australia's money comes from the work these people do.

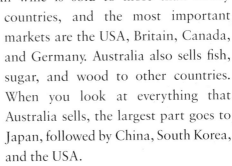

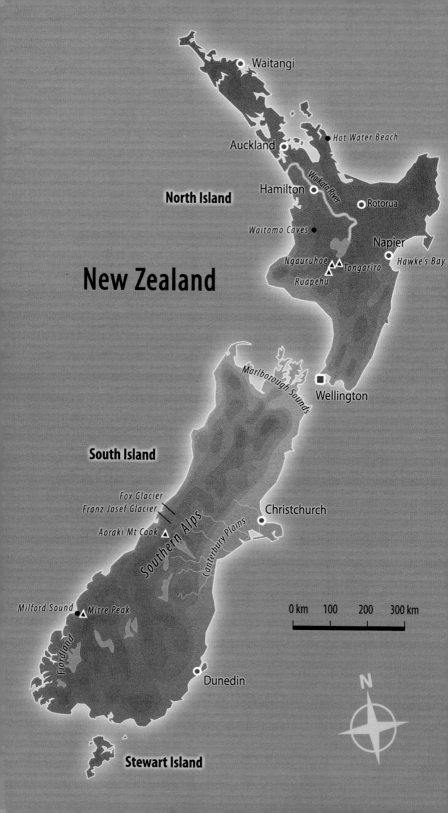

7   A faraway land

New Zealand is a long way from everywhere – three hours by plane from Australia, and about twenty-six hours by plane from Britain. It is a country of islands; the North Island and the South Island are the main ones, and there are many smaller ones.

It is a long, narrow country; nowhere in New Zealand is more than 130 kilometres from the sea. It is a little larger than Great Britain, but Great Britain has a population of 60 million, and New Zealand has just 4.1 million people. It is an exciting and surprising land; as well as mountains, forests, lakes, deserts, and rivers, there are places where hot water and steam explode out of the ground.

The weather in New Zealand is usually not too hot and not too cold. There is lots of sun, but plenty of rain, and the weather often changes quickly too. The hottest months are from December to February, when it is usually between 20 and 30 °C, and the coldest months are June to August, when it is between 10 and 15 °C. The warmest part of New Zealand is the north of the North Island.

It is a young country too. Nobody lived there until the first Māori people landed there about a thousand years ago, and the first British people came to live there around 1840. The oldest tree in New Zealand is more than 1,200 years old, but you will not find any buildings that are more than about 200 years old. And in New Zealand today more than half the people are under thirty-four years old.

If you travel from the top of the North Island to the

Beautiful beaches . . .

bottom of the South Island – a journey of 2,000 kilometres – you will see a lot of different kinds of countryside. In the north it is warm enough to grow oranges, and there are dozens of little islands and beautiful beaches. South of the city of Auckland you travel through the green hills near the Waikato River to the centre of the North Island. Here there is a group of three high volcanoes, Ruapehu, Ngauruhoe, and Tongariro. Sometimes fire and steam come out of these mountains; this happened in 1996, and again in 2006. The North Island's main rivers, the Waikato, Wanganui, Rangitikei, and Rangitaiki, all begin near the centre of the island; water from the Waikato, which is 425 kilometres long, makes electricity for New Zealand.

In the South Island the mountains called

the Southern Alps go almost from one end of the island to the other. Near the centre of the island is New Zealand's highest mountain, Aoraki Mount Cook, which is 3,754 metres high. There are many lakes and rivers on the east side of the mountains, and it is a very popular place for sport – skiing in the winter, and water sports on the lakes in the summer. Between the mountains and the east coast are the Canterbury Plains – wide flat land where there are a lot of farms.

On the other side of the island is the wild west coast. Few people live here now, but once thousands came here looking for gold. Continue south and you come to Fiordland. Here you can travel by boat along Milford Sound, 16 kilometres of deep water with thick forest on each side and the beautiful mountain of Mitre Peak at the end. Your journey from the top to the bottom of New Zealand ends at Stewart Island, or Rakiura, New Zealand's third island. It is a good place to see the Southern Lights, beautiful red and green colours in the night sky.

Mitre Peak above Milford Sound

8   New Zealand's past

About one thousand years ago the first Māori came to New Zealand. They travelled from islands in the Pacific Ocean to the country that they called Aotearoa – the land of the long white cloud. At first they lived in both islands, but later they lived mainly on the coasts and rivers of the North Island.

In 1642 the Dutch sailor Abel Tasman visited New Zealand and gave it its name, from Zeeland ('Sea Land') which is a part of the Netherlands. Captain James Cook visited the islands four times between 1769 and 1777, sailed all the way round them and made the first map of the country. In 1840 Captain William Hobson wrote the Treaty of Waitangi. This said that the queen of Great Britain, Queen Victoria, was now queen of New Zealand too. About 40 Māori chiefs agreed to this, and later another 500 did so. But when more British people came to live in New Zealand, fighting about the land began between the Māori and the British. The fighting finally ended in about 1870.

In 1863 gold was found in the South Island, and thousands of people hurried to New Zealand to look for gold. Later, thousands more people came from Britain to the new country. In 1871, the white population was 250,000; ten years later it was 500,000. New Zealand became a kind of big British farm, sending meat, butter, and cheese back to Britain by ship.

The young country was not afraid to try new things. In 1893, New Zealand was the first country in the world to let women vote. In the 1930s, the New Zealand government decided that all schools and hospitals should be free for all its people. And in 1987 New Zealand became a nuclear-free zone. This means that ships that use nuclear power or carry nuclear bombs cannot come into New Zealand waters, and that the country does not use nuclear power to make electricity.

Women going to vote in 1893

New Zealand soldiers fought in both World Wars beside British and American soldiers, and most New Zealanders felt that they were still part of the great family of countries that once belonged to Britain. But there have been big changes in the country since the 1950s. From the 1950s to the 1970s, many immigrants came to New Zealand from Pacific islands like Tonga and Samoa, often to work in factories. And from the 1980s, New Zealand began to look first at the jobs that immigrants could do, instead of the country that they came from. This opened the doors to many people who had not been able to move to New Zealand before. Today, a quarter of a million people from Pacific islands live in New Zealand, and a quarter of a million from Asian countries.

Between March 2005 and August 2006, something new and interesting happened in New Zealand – women had the five most important jobs in the country. One of the five women was Queen Elizabeth the Second (who is queen of New Zealand), and two others were Helen Clark, the prime minister, and Dame Sian Elias, the country's top judge. It is the first time that this has happened anywhere in the world.

9   Five cities

Auckland, the most northern of New Zealand's four main cities, has the biggest population; 1.2 million people live there. It is the biggest city too; to get from one end of Auckland to the other you need to travel more than 50 kilometres. Auckland has two harbours, the Manukau on the west coast and the Waitemata on the east coast; at the narrowest part of the city it is only 1.5 kilometres from one harbour to the other. Many people in Auckland like sailing,

Auckland from the Waitemata harbour

and on fine days Aucklanders love to swim and sail in the harbour. One of Auckland's names is 'the City of Sails'.

Auckland has a modern business centre with many tall buildings. Visitors like to go to the top of the Sky Tower, in the centre of the city; it is 328 metres high, and from there you can see the two harbours and many islands near Auckland's coast. People from all over the world live in the city, and it has the biggest population of people from the Pacific islands of any city in the world.

Wellington, at the southern end of the North Island, has a population of 370,000. Although it is not the largest city, it is the capital, because it is close to the centre of the country, and the New Zealand government meets there. Wellington is built on high hills around a lovely harbour and has lots of good shops and restaurants. It is also a centre for film, music, and theatre. Parts of *The Lord of the Rings* (2001–2003) were filmed in and around Wellington, and you can take a tour by bus to see these places.

Christchurch is the South Island's largest city with 367,000 people. It is a flat, green place; one third of the city is parks and gardens, and it is called the 'Garden City'. To many people Christchurch is 'the most English city outside England'; it was designed in England, and its river is called the Avon.

The fourth city is Dunedin, which is the old name for Edinburgh in Scotland. In the nineteenth century it was the centre of New Zealand's business and its largest city, and many of Dunedin's most beautiful buildings were built at this time. It also has New Zealand's oldest university, and the 'steepest street in the world'! Baldwin Street is short but very steep, and every year there is a race to the top of the street and down again. It is, in fact, harder to run down Baldwin Street than up it.

And now there is a fifth important city. Hamilton is about 130 kilometres south of Auckland, and it has a bigger population than Dunedin. It is in the centre of some of New Zealand's richest farmland, and the Waikato River goes through the centre of the city. It is growing quickly, and many immigrants choose Hamilton as a place to live.

Baldwin Street, Dunedin

10   Māori

Māori have lived in New Zealand for more than a thousand years. When Captain Cook and his men landed there, they found a tall, strong people with brown skin and black hair. Māori of those times lived in wooden houses and had wooden boats, and they often cut beautiful shapes into the wood which they worked with. They caught birds and fish and grew sweet potatoes for food. They were also excellent singers and dancers. They were called tangata whenua ('people of the land') because the land was a very important part of their lives. At this time the Māori population was between 100,000 and 150,000.

When the British came it was, in many ways, not a good thing for Māori. Many people, both Māori and Pākehā (the Māori name for white people) died in the battles over land. People still argue today about the land and who owns it, and many people feel very strongly about it. The Pākehā also brought guns, alcohol, and cigarettes with them, and diseases which were new to Māori. All of these things brought terrible trouble to Māori, and many of them died. By 1900 the future seemed hopeless, and the Māori population was down to 50,000, but after a while the population slowly began to grow again.

In the twentieth century many Māori began to live more like the Pākehā. Sir Apirana Ngata, for example, was successful in the Māori world, where he studied the stories, songs, and language of his people, and in the Pākehā world, where he worked in the New Zealand government. But not all the changes were good. Many Māori families left their old homes and moved to the cities, so the old Māori way of life began to die. And the Māori language was dying with it, because Māori children had to speak English, not Māori, at school.

But in the 1960s and 1970s many Māori, especially young ones, began to think seriously about the future. They began to learn the Māori language, and to learn more about the Māori way of life. People began to ask questions about Māori land too. Many Māori argued that the Treaty of Waitangi meant different things to Māori and Pākehā, and this meant that Māori had lost land that really belonged to them.

In 1981 the South African rugby team planned to come to New Zealand. Teams from South Africa had visited many

times before, but this time was different. Many New Zealanders – both Māori and Pākehā – became angry. They did not want New Zealand teams to play against the South Africans, who only chose white players to play for their country, and who did not welcome Māori players into South Africa. But the New Zealand government refused to stop the South African rugby team from playing in New Zealand. People argued about this all over the country; there were some angry fights, and some matches were stopped.

People were realizing that Māori were an important part of New Zealand, and things began to change. Since 1975 the Waitangi Tribunal has listened to arguments about land and decided what should happen. There are more than 500 kohanga reo – schools where very young children begin to learn Māori – and both Māori and Pākehā can learn the language at school. Māori is an official language, and there are Māori radio and TV stations. Some government offices

Māori dancers

Māori march for land rights

work in both languages, and some place names have changed. For example, New Zealand's highest mountain was once called Mount Cook; today it is known as Aoraki Mount Cook, with its Māori and English names used together.

Today there are about 526,000 Māori people in New Zealand – that is about 15 per cent of the population. There are still problems for Māori; many of them have worse health than Pākehā, and it is more difficult for them to finish school, get good jobs, and find good houses. And now there are many other people – from the Pacific islands, Asian countries, and countries in Europe – who want a place in New Zealand as well. But Māori are sure to be an important part of New Zealand's future. Although they nearly disappeared a hundred years ago, today their voice is becoming stronger again.

11 Wonders of New Zealand

Let's begin in Auckland. Visitors to the city often do not realize that Auckland's hills are volcanoes – all forty-eight of them. The youngest one is Rangitoto, which came up out of the sea only 600 years ago. But there is no danger from these volcanoes now; they have been quiet for years.

The strangest place in New Zealand is surely Rotorua, a city near the centre of the North Island. Here the air smells like eggs, and hot water explodes out of the ground. You can walk beside lakes of hot water of extraordinary colours, and there are pools of natural hot water where you can swim. Near Rotorua, steam is used to make electricity.

Not far away at Hot Water Beach on the Coromandel Peninsula you can find hot water coming up through the sand next to the cold sea. Visitors like to dig in the sand and make themselves a pool of hot water to lie in.

About 150 kilometres west of Rotorua are the Waitomo Caves. These enormous caves were made by a river. The best part of a visit is a journey along the river in a boat; you travel silently through the darkness of the caves until suddenly you see thousands of little stars above you. In fact these stars are lights; they belong to very small animals, like flies, which live on the roof of the cave.

In 1931 an earthquake destroyed much of the city of Napier, on the east coast of the North Island. When the new city was built, it was in the Art Deco style that was popular

A lake at Rotorua

at the time. Now there are only two places in the world where you can see a lot of Art Deco buildings – Napier, and South Beach in Florida, USA. Some of Napier's Art Deco buildings were knocked down in the 1960s and 1970s, but many of them are still there, and a lot of visitors come to Napier to see them.

The Fox Glacier

At the northern end of the South Island there are the Marlborough Sounds. They were once river valleys, but now the valleys are below the sea. Captain Cook came here in the 1770s, and if you travel by boat from the North Island to the South Island you will go through the Marlborough Sounds. The sounds are full of forests, islands, and beautiful beaches, and it is a great place to sail, walk, or cycle.

On the west coast of the South Island are the Franz Josef and Fox Glaciers. The Fox Glacier is 13 kilometres long and drops 2,600 metres from the mountains of the Southern Alps to the sea. You can walk to the bottom of the glaciers and see these great rivers of blue ice from close up, or you can take a plane to the top of the glacier.

In the south-west of the South Island is Fiordland, where land and sea meet in deep valleys. Many visitors like to walk along the Milford Track. This walk takes four days, and on the way you can stop to see the Sutherland Falls, which are 580 metres high. When you arrive at Milford Sound at the end of your walk you can take a boat trip and see the mountains and forests from the water.

12 Ten sheep and two cows

With warm temperatures and a lot of rain, New Zealand is a great place for farms of all kinds. Sheep and cows are found on farms in both the North and South Islands; the oldest farms began in the middle of the nineteenth century. Until the 1940s people said that New Zealanders 'lived off the sheep's back'; in other words, the country made most of its money from the wool and meat from its sheep, which it sold mostly to the UK. At that time one person in four worked on a farm.

Now only one person in ten works on a farm, but there are still a lot of animals. For every person living in New Zealand there are ten sheep and two cows – or about 40 million sheep and 8 million cows in the whole country. There are other farm animals too, of course, like chickens.

A lot of fruit is grown here too – apples, for example, and more recently kiwifruit. Before the 1970s not many people knew kiwifruit outside New Zealand and China; now millions of the small brown fruit are sent all over the world from farms in the North Island.

As well as New Zealand trees like rimu, totara and kauri, which cover more than a quarter of the land, other trees are also grown for wood and paper. In the centre of the North Island there are large forests of trees that are cut and used in New Zealand and sold to other countries too.

People have made wine in New Zealand for a hundred

Some of the 40 million sheep

years, but since the 1970s it has become much more popular, both in New Zealand and outside it. It is made in many parts of the country, but Hawke's Bay in the east of the North Island and Marlborough at the top of the South Island are especially famous for their wine.

New Zealand also sells a lot of fish, especially to Asian countries. And New Zealanders are always looking for new things that they can grow and sell; grapes and flowers are some of the new things on the New Zealand market.

13 Free time and sport

Both Australia and New Zealand have plenty of space and good weather, so naturally people spend a lot of their free time outside. Although there are flats in cities, most people like to live in a house of their own with a garden. Families spend hours in their gardens, growing flowers and vegetables, playing and having meals.

Barbecues are popular, and New Zealanders like a hangi too. This is a Māori way of cooking. You make a fire in a hole in the ground, and then put stones on top of the fire. When the stones are hot, you put meat and vegetables on top of the stones, throw on water, cover the food, and fill up the hole. After two or three hours you uncover the food and lift it out – and it tastes wonderful!

Taking food out of a hangi

Australian rules football

Until the middle of the twentieth century meals in both countries were very much like British meals, and people usually sat down in the evening to eat meat, potatoes, and vegetables. But now people travel more, and immigrants have brought new foods and new ways of cooking. Young cooks are interested in cooking unusual foods – kangaroo meat, for example, or New Zealand fish – together with foods from Asian or European countries.

Playing (and watching) sport is a very important part of life in both countries. Australia has had the Olympic Games twice; Sydney was home to the very successful Summer Olympics in 2000. Water sports are especially popular because so many people live near to the sea (and in 10 per cent of Australian gardens there is a swimming pool). Almost everyone learns to swim, and Australia has had some great swimmers. The most recent was Ian Thorpe, who began swimming for Australia at the age of fourteen, and later won six Olympic gold medals. Sailing is also popular, and in summer the harbours are full of boats, big and small. In 1995 and 2000 New Zealand beat some of the best boats in the world to win the America's Cup, the world's top sailing race.

If you like football, you will find four different kinds of football to play or watch in Australia and New Zealand. There is soccer – the game known as 'football' in many countries – and rugby league, which is also played in England and some European countries. But the most popular kind in Australia is Australian rules football. More than half a million people in Australia play this fast, exciting game with as many as eighteen players on each team. On the day of the final match, in Melbourne in September each year, everything stops in Australia, and millions of people watch the game.

In New Zealand the most popular kind of football is rugby. The New Zealand team is called the All Blacks. Before a game of rugby, the All Blacks do a haka – a Māori dance that makes them feel strong and tries to frighten the other team. It must work, because they are the most successful team in history!

Many other sports are popular – tennis, running, netball, and golf are some of them. Thousands of people like to go to watch horse races, and many of them hope to win some money too. The biggest race of all is the Melbourne Cup, which is held in Melbourne every year in November. That day is a holiday in Melbourne, and all over Australia everything stops when the race begins. Millions of people watch the race on TV or listen to it on the radio. Thousands of New Zealanders watch the race as well – and sometimes the winning horse is from New Zealand!

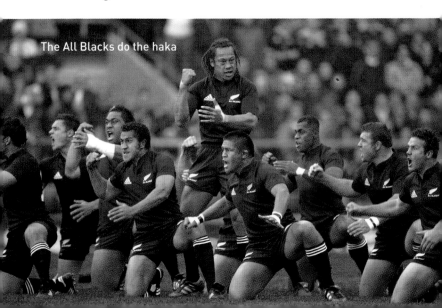

The All Blacks do the haka

14 Animals, birds, and plants

Why are there so many extraordinary animals, birds, and plants in Australia and New Zealand? Until recently, it was not easy for people or animals to reach these two countries, so nothing changed quickly there. Many Australian animals are not found in any other country, and the same is true of many birds and plants from both countries.

The kangaroo is one Australian animal that everybody knows. The biggest of the fifty different kinds is the red kangaroo. They have big strong back legs and tails, and an adult can be 2.4 metres high. They can jump more than 4 metres and travel at 70 kilometres an hour. Kangaroos eat grass and leaves and live in groups of about twelve.

Everyone loves the sleepy grey koalas. Like kangaroos, they have a pouch (a kind of pocket) on their fronts for their babies; after six months here, a baby koala rides on its mother's back. They live in eucalyptus trees, sleeping for eighteen hours and eating 1 kilo of leaves each day, but they drink almost nothing.

In the seas and rivers of northern Australia you can find crocodiles that are 5 or 6 metres long. They eat fish, animals, kangaroos – and sometimes people.

Finally, two very strange animals – the echidna and the platypus. Their babies are born from eggs but drink milk from their mothers; no other animals in the world do this. The echidna catches its food with its long fast tongue. The

A platypus

platypus has a wide flat tail. It swims well, but it can only stay under water for a few minutes, and it shuts its eyes and ears first.

There are more than 800 kinds of bird in Australia. The emu, which is 2 metres tall, is the second largest bird in the world; only the ostrich is bigger. It cannot fly at all, but it can run at 50 kilometres an hour. Then there is the kookaburra, whose cry sounds like someone laughing, and the budgerigar, a little blue or yellow bird that people keep in their homes all over the world. Finally, there is the wonderful lyrebird. These birds live on the ground and have beautiful long tails. They have their own songs, but they can also sing the songs of other birds, and they can make the sounds of things like a car engine, the click of a camera, and a crying baby!

Eucalyptus trees are found everywhere in Australia, and one kind, the great mountain ash, can grow to 92 metres. These strong trees do not die when there are forest fires. Australia has many other kinds of tree, and thousands of kinds of wild flower too.

No wild animals lived on the land before people arrived in New Zealand. Because of this, some New Zealand birds lived on the ground without danger, and one of these was the kiwi. The kiwi does have wings, but they have become very small, so it cannot fly. It cannot see very well either – but it can smell, and not many birds can do that. Many people recognize this strange bird now, and New Zealanders are often called Kiwis.

The kakapo is another New Zealand bird that cannot fly – but it is very good at climbing. Kakapos are large, heavy, green birds that come out at night to look for food. There are only eighty-six kakapos alive in the world today, so New Zealanders have made special places for them to live. These are on islands where there are no people, cats, dogs, or other animals that could kill the birds. Everyone hopes that soon there will be more kakapos.

New Zealand is also the home of the tuatara, which lives on a few small islands off the coast. The tuatara is one of the oldest types of animal in the world, and it has not really changed for 200 million years. Tuatara are about 60 centimetres long and have a third 'eye' on the top of their

A tuatara

heads. They sleep during the winter, and they use the third eye to wake themselves up in spring.

Finally, New Zealand has many beautiful trees. The pohutukawa tree has red flowers at Christmas time, and people call it the 'New Zealand Christmas tree'. But the greatest tree of them all is the kauri. Kauris are tall, straight

Tane Mahuta, the great kauri

trees, and their wood is excellent for boats, bridges, furniture, and houses. Today you cannot cut down kauri trees, but you can visit the kauri forests to see these wonderful trees. The tallest kauri in New Zealand is in the Waipoua forest, north of Auckland. It is called Tane Mahuta, or king of the forest; it is 52 metres tall, and more than 1,500 years old.

15 Famous people

Ned Kelly

One of the earliest and most famous Australians is Ned Kelly. Together with his brother and two other men, Kelly robbed banks in the 1870s. Kelly and his friends wore armour which they made themselves, and they soon became famous all over Australia. Kelly was finally caught and killed in 1880, when he was just twenty-five. A famous group of paintings by Sir Sidney Nolan shows Ned Kelly and his men. You can read the story of Ned Kelly in *Ned Kelly: A True Story* (Oxford Bookworms Stage 1).

Australia has had a lot of sports stars too. In tennis Rod Laver won four times in the 1960s at Wimbledon in London, where international tennis stars play every year to find the best players in the world. Pat Cash won there once, and Margaret Court won three times between 1963 and 1970. Evonne Goolagong won at Wimbledon in 1971, and then again in 1980, and was perhaps the first Aborigine to be famous through sport. The young player Lleyton Hewitt was the number one men's player in the world in 2001 at the age of twenty, and won at Wimbledon in 2002.

As well as Ian Thorpe, Australia has had other swimming stars. One of them was Shane Gould, who won three

Cathy Freeman

Olympic gold medals at the age of fifteen. In cricket, Steve Waugh and Shane Warne are names that are known in Australia and the rest of the world. But one of the most popular sportspeople of recent years was the Aboriginal runner Cathy Freeman. Cathy won the 400 metres race at the Sydney Olympics in 2000, and Australians of all kinds and colours were excited by her success.

Kerry Packer, a businessman who owned newspapers, television stations, and a lot of land, was possibly the richest person in Australia when he died in 2005. International businessman Rupert Murdoch started *The Australian*, the first daily newspaper for all Australia, in 1964, and now has businesses in Australia, the USA, Great Britain, and Hong Kong.

Patrick White wrote *The Tree of Man* and *Voss*, and won the Nobel Prize in 1973. Thomas Keneally's book *Schindler's Ark* later became the successful film *Schindler's List*. Other popular Australian writers are Peter Carey, Germaine Greer, and Robert Hughes.

The film star Mel Gibson is famous for the *Lethal Weapon* and *Mad Max* films and *Braveheart*, and more recently *The Passion of the Christ*. But now Russell Crowe is Australia's biggest film star, after he won an Oscar for *Gladiator* (though Crowe was in fact born in New Zealand). Nicole Kidman and Cate Blanchett have both had international success; in 2006 Kidman was the highest paid woman in films. And at the top of the list of singers must be Kylie Minogue. She began on television, but is now known all over the world as a singer and dancer.

Finally among the Australians, there are two very unusual people. Steve Irwin grew up working with crocodiles and other animals. Later he appeared on television and made films about wild animals in Australia and other countries. Sadly, he died in an accident while making a film at the Great Barrier Reef in 2006. And international television star Edna Everage, with her extraordinary clothes, purple hair, and fantastic sunglasses, could only come from Australia. Dame Edna has appeared on television shows since the 1960s, and she even has a street named after her – Dame Edna Place – in Melbourne. (In fact, Dame Edna is really a man called Barry Humphries.)

Who is the most famous New Zealander of all? In the twentieth century, the answer was probably Sir Edmund Hillary. On 29 May 1953, Hillary stood on top of Mount Everest with the Nepalese climber Tenzing Norgay – the first people in the world to do so. Later Hillary returned to Nepal to work with the people of Nepal and he helped to build schools and hospitals there.

Bill Hamilton loved cars, boats and engines, and he

Edmund Hillary and Tenzing Norgay

wanted a boat that could travel fast on the shallow rivers of the South Island. So he invented the Hamilton Jetboat. In 1960 four of these boats travelled 160 kilometres up the Colorado River in the USA, and soon people were buying jetboats all over the world.

New Zealand has its sports stars too. In the 1960s Arthur Lydiard began teaching young runners. Two of them, Peter Snell and Murray Halberg, went on to win gold medals in the Olympics. Bruce McLaren had international success as a racing car driver in the 1960s, and McLaren drivers have continued to win prizes since then.

Every New Zealander can tell you stories about their favourite All Black, but one that everybody knows is Jonah Lomu. Tall (1.96 metres), heavy (119 kilos), fast and strong, Lomu played 73 times for the All Blacks between 1994 and 2002, and many people think that he was the first international rugby star. Sailor Sir Peter Blake was another favourite sportsman. He won the Whitbread Round the World race in 1989, and then managed the New Zealand sailors that won

Peter Jackson

the America's Cup twice. Sadly, he was murdered while sailing on the Amazon in 2001.

Some other twentieth century New Zealanders are Sir Peter Buck (Te Rangi Hiroa), who was the first Māori doctor, and who studied the Māori way of life; Ernest Rutherford, who won the Nobel Prize for his scientific work; and Katherine Mansfield, who wrote excellent short stories. Dame Kiri Te Kanawa became famous as a singer and sang at the wedding of Prince Charles and Diana, Princess of Wales in St Paul's Cathedral, London.

Perhaps the most famous New Zealander today is Peter Jackson. Jackson loved films as a child and began making them while still young. In the late 1990s he started work on the three films of *The Lord of the Rings*, and they were enormously successful. The three films together won seventeen Oscars. Jackson then made a new film of *King Kong*, which was also very successful. Although he is famous, Jackson still lives and works in New Zealand, and the three *Lord of the Rings* films were first shown there. He also has a small part in all of his films; in *King Kong* he tries to shoot the animal from a plane.

16 Today and tomorrow

In both Australia and New Zealand you can find British and Aboriginal or Māori things side by side. To the people who live there, this is natural, but it sometimes seems surprising to visitors. In Australia you can find very British place names like Melbourne, Brighton, and Liverpool next to Aboriginal place names like Mullumbimby, Wagga Wagga, and Goondiwindi; in New Zealand British place names like Palmerston North and Hamilton are found with Māori place names like Ngaruawahia and Wanganui.

Once many white people talked about 'home' and meant Britain, but that does not happen often now. People remember

Christmas in Australia

Bungee jumping in New Zealand

the past, but they add new things from the new countries. For example, at Christmas many people come together to sing Christmas songs, but because it is summer they can do this outside in summer clothes. Lots of people have a cold meal at Christmas, and quite often they will eat it outside or at the beach – but some people have a big hot Christmas dinner in July, when the weather is colder!

Other things are changing too. Australia began its modern life as a place where Britain could send its convicts. Now it is a place that people want to visit; about 5 million tourists come to Australia every year, and nearly 400,000 of them are young people from Britain, the USA, and Europe. New Zealand began as a big farm growing food for Britain, and until the 1960s more than half of New Zealand's money came from sales to the UK. Today those sales are worth only 5 per cent; New Zealand's main customer now is Australia, and then the USA, Japan, and China.

And Australians and New Zealanders are always looking for new things to do, make, or sell. Before the 1970s, for example, it was hard to think of the name of a film from Australia or New Zealand. But since then, people have made hundreds of films in both countries, and films like *Shine* and *Crocodile Dundee* from Australia, and *The Piano* and *Whale Rider* from New Zealand, have had international success.

Think about bungee jumping too. In this sport you jump from a high place, like a bridge, and fall a long way before a rope pulls you back up again. New Zealander A. J. Hackett thought that he could make a business from this, and he made a special rope for the job. In 1987 he showed bungee jumping to the world when he jumped off the Eiffel Tower in Paris – and now there are more places to go bungee jumping in New Zealand than in any other country. Now, on the roads that farmers drove along to reach their South Island farms, you will see tourists. Perhaps they are driving to bridges where they can go bungee jumping, or visiting places that they saw in the films of *The Lord of the Rings*.

In the past young Australians and New Zealanders often

went travelling to Britain and Europe for a year or two when they finished studying. Many still do, but others also go to countries like Thailand, China, and Japan. Often these young people are as interested in their own country and its neighbours as they are in Britain on the other side of the world. In 1999 the government of Australia asked its people, 'Do you want Australia to be a republic, with a president instead of a queen?' Although 55 per cent of Australians said no, many people think that one day Australia will say yes, and then the Queen (or King) of the United Kingdom will no longer be the Queen (or King) of Australia. When that happens, perhaps New Zealand will do the same.

You cannot just get in your car or onto a train and go to Australia or New Zealand – it takes a long time (and quite a lot of money) to get there. But that is one of the things that make these two countries so special. Kangaroos, kiwis, Uluru, geysers, underground houses and kiwifruit, and some of the friendliest people in the world – they are all waiting for you 'down under'. Why not come and see for yourself?

GLOSSARY

alcohol strong drinks like wine, beer, or whisky

armour metal 'clothes' to protect your body when you are fighting

base a place where soldiers live and work

camel a large animal with one or two round parts on its back that lives in hot dry places

cattle cows that are kept for their milk or meat

cave a large hole in the side of a mountain or under the ground

convict a person who has been sent to prison for doing something wrong

coral reef a long line of rocks in the sea that are made from the bones of very small animals

countryside land with fields, forests, farms etc, that is away from towns and cities

desert a large, dry area of land with very few plants

design to draw a plan that shows how to make something

earthquake a sudden strong shaking of the ground

electricity power that can make heat and light

enormous very big

especially more than usual or more than others

festival a series of events, for example music or films, held in one place

government a group of people who control a country

harbour a place where ships can stay safely in the water

immigrant a person who comes to another country to live there

international connected with two or more countries

Internet the international network of computers that lets you see information from all over the world

jetboat a fast boat that can travel on a few centimetres of water

judge the person in court who decides how to punish somebody

medal a piece of metal with words and pictures on it that you get for doing something very good

mineral things like coal, oil, gold and salt that come from the
    ground and that people use

nuclear power energy made by splitting atoms

oil a thick liquid from under the ground that we use for energy

Olympic Games an international sports festival that is organized
    every four years in a different country

Oscar one of the awards given every year in the USA for the best
    film, actor etc

paint to put coloured liquid on something to change its colour

pool a place that is made for people to swim in

population the number of people who live in a place

power the ability to control people or things

race a competition to see who can run, drive etc. the fastest

road train a large lorry pulling extra parts, like a train with
    carriages

rope very thick strong string

state a part of a country with its own government

steam the gas that water becomes when it gets very hot

steep a steep hill goes up quickly from a low place to a high
    place

style a way of doing something

team a group of people who play a sport together against
    another group

temperature how hot or cold a place is

volcano a mountain with a hole in the top where fire and gas
    sometimes come out

vote to choose somebody in an election

war fighting between armies of different countries

wheat a kind of grain that can be made into flour

wine an alcoholic drink made from grapes

wonder something that is strange, surprising, or beautiful

Australia and New Zealand

ACTIVITIES

ACTIVITIES

Before Reading

1 Match the words to the pictures. You can use a dictionary.

barbecue / geyser / glacier / kangaroo / koala / sailing

Which of these pictures belong to Australia? Which belong to New Zealand? Which could belong to both countries?

2 How much do you know about Australia and New Zealand? Three of these sentences are true – which ones are they?

1 Australia is smaller than Canada.
2 Less than half of all Australians live in cities.
3 In New Zealand you are never more than 130 kilometres from the sea.
4 The hottest months in Australia and New Zealand are from December to February.
5 Auckland is the capital of New Zealand.
6 There are more cows than sheep in New Zealand.

ACTIVITIES

While Reading

Read Chapters 1 and 2. Are these sentences true (T) or false (F)? Rewrite the false sentences to make them true.

1 Western Australia is bigger than Texas. T/ F
2 Most of Australia gets a lot of rain. T/ F
3 In Australia Christmas is in the winter. T/ F
4 Most Australians do not live far from the sea. T/ F
5 The Aborigines arrived in Australia after the Chinese. T/ F
6 The first British people to live in Australia were convicts. T/ F
7 When oil was found, the population grew quickly. T/ F
8 Many people moved to Australia before the Second World War. T/ F

Read Chapter 3, then circle the correct words.

1 Sydney's harbour is one of the *deepest / largest* in the world.
2 Melbourne *is / was* the capital of Australia.
3 South Australia is famous for its *wine / fruit*.
4 Perth is a good place to visit if you like the *sea / snow*.
5 There are no tall buildings in Darwin because of the *weather / cost*.
6 Canberra was planned by an *Aborigine / American*.
7 The outback has *more / fewer* people than Hobart.
8 Cattle are taken from the stations by *plane / road train*.
9 *Tourists / teachers* bring a lot of business to Alice Springs.
10 In the outback you can travel by *kangaroo / camel* if you want to.
11 When you travel in the outback, you must take plenty of *clothes / water*.

Read Chapters 4, 5, and 6. Choose the best question-word for these questions, and then answer them.

How, What, Where, Which, Why

1   . . . did the Aborigines think that the world began?
2   . . . problems do Aborigines have in Australia today?
3   . . . did Australians have National Sorry Day?
4   . . . happens to Uluru when the sun goes down?
5   . . . do people live underground in Coober Pedy?
6   . . . is unusual about the boats at the Todd River Regatta?
7   . . . do merino sheep do well in Australia?
8   . . . are oil and minerals found in Australia?
9   . . . country is Australia's best customer?

Read Chapters 7 and 8. Fill in the gaps with these words.

Alps, Asian, centre, electricity, first, gold, highest, lowest, map, name, Pacific, River, sailor, southern, volcanoes, west, women

1   The temperature is _____ between June and August, and the _____ part of the country is colder than the north.
2   There are three _____ in the _____ of the North Island.
3   The Waikato _____ is used to make _____.
4   Aoraki Mount Cook, in the Southern _____, is New Zealand's _____ mountain.
5   On the _____ side of the South Island people once looked for _____.
6   A Dutch _____ gave New Zealand its _____, but a British captain made the first _____.
7   New Zealand was the _____ country to let _____ vote.
8   More than 10 per cent of New Zealand's population come from _____ Islands and _____ countries.

Read Chapters 9 and 10. Change these untrue sentences to true sentences.

1 Auckland has a high mountain in the centre of the city.

2 Wellington is at the northern end of the South Island.

3 Christchurch is called the 'City of Sails'.

4 Dunedin gets its name from a Māori city.

5 Hamilton is on the coast.

6 Māori came to New Zealand a hundred years ago.

7 Pākehā is the name that Māori give to their children.

8 There was trouble in 1981 because the New Zealand rugby team went to South Africa.

9 The Waitangi Tribunal makes decisions about the Māori language.

Read Chapters 11 and 12. Match the places with the things you find there.

1 Auckland	a) river valleys below the sea
2 Rotorua	b) natural hot water
3 Napier	c) wine
4 The Marlborough Sounds	d) the Sutherland Falls
5 Fiordland	e) kiwifruit
6 North Island farms	f) volcanoes
7 Hawke's Bay	g) Art Deco buildings

Read Chapters 13 and 14. Match these halves of sentences.

1 Because many people have a garden, . . .
2 At a hangi you eat food. . .
3 Because people live near the sea and the weather is good . . .
4 Before the All Blacks play a game of rugby . . .
5 Crocodiles usually eat fish and small animals . . .
6 Emus cannot fly . . .
7 Tuataras sleep during the winter . . .
8 Tane Mahuta began to grow . . .

a) they try to frighten the other team with a haka.
b) and their third eye wakes them up in spring.
c) that has been cooked in the ground on hot stones.
d) before Māori came to New Zealand.
e) swimming and sailing are both popular.
f) but they can run nearly as fast as a kangaroo.
g) they spend a lot of time outside.
h) but sometimes they eat people as well.

Read Chapters 15 and 16, then circle the correct words.

1 Pat Cash and Lleyton Hewitt were *tennis/swimming* stars.
2 Patrick White won an *Olympic medal / the Nobel Prize*.
3 Kylie Minogue is a famous Australian *singer / artist*.
4 Jonah Lomu is famous for *playing rugby / sailing*.
5 Peter Jackson's first big success was *King Kong / The Lord of the Rings*.
6 At Christmas, people usually prefer to eat *hot / cold* food.
7 New Zealand sells *more / less* to Australia than to the UK.
8 Many people think that in the future *more / fewer* Australians will decide that they want Australia to be a republic.

ACTIVITIES

After Reading

1 Here are two e-mails, one from Australia, and one from New Zealand. Complete them using the words below (one word for each gap).

Aboriginal, bungee, camel, coast, crocodiles, fun, gold, hope, jetboat, looks, purple, screamed, snow, sun, terribly

---

From: Corinne
Subject: Hello from Aoraki Mount Cook!

Today I went for a _____ ride. It went very fast and I _____ a lot and got very wet! There is a lot of _____ here on the mountain, and the countryside is really beautiful. Tomorrow I'm going to go _____ jumping from a bridge over one of the rivers. It _____ frightening to me, but everybody says that it's _____. Then on Friday I'm off to the west _____. Perhaps I can find some _____!

Bye!
Corinne

From: Marco
Subject: Hi from the outback

It's _____ hot here, but it's really interesting too. I stayed near Uluru last week. When the _____ went down the rock looked so beautiful – every colour from gold to _____. Tomorrow I'm planning to go on a _____ ride. We're going to see some _____ paintings, and then we'll go down to a river. I _____ there aren't any _____!

See you soon.
Marco

2   Find these words in the word search below. The words go
    from left to right and top to bottom.

*camel, cattle, cave, convict, coral reef, countryside, desert,
electricity, harbour, immigrant, jetboat, judge, nuclear power,
oil, pool, steam, volcano*

A	Y	N	J	E	T	B	O	A	T	N
E	C	O	N	V	I	C	T	U	S	U
L	L	V	O	L	C	A	N	O	D	C
E	P	R	I	Z	O	C	A	M	E	L
C	O	U	N	T	R	Y	S	I	D	E
T	O	S	T	E	A	M	E	B	C	A
R	L	O	M	Q	L	V	T	Q	A	R
I	M	M	I	G	R	A	N	T	V	P
C	A	T	T	L	E	H	F	W	E	O
I	R	O	R	D	E	S	E	R	T	W
T	P	I	O	A	F	J	U	D	G	E
Y	I	L	G	H	A	R	B	O	U	R

Put the words into groups under these four headings.

ALIVE	WATER	LAND	POWER
_____	_____	_____	_____
_____	_____	_____	_____
_____	_____	_____	_____
_____	_____	_____	_____
_____	_____	_____	_____

3 Read these paragraphs and choose the right answers to make two texts, one about the Aborigines and one about Māori.

The Aborigines / Māori came to *New Zealand / Australia* about *40,000 / 1,000* years ago. They lived in houses made from *branches / wood*, and caught *birds / animals* and fish. They were good at singing and dancing, and they *painted their bodies / made beautiful wooden boats.*

When the British came, many died in fights over land or from diseases. In the twentieth century things changed for *Māori / the Aborigines.* They *began to live more like / had to live separately from* the white people. Now most of them live in cities and towns, and they are about *15 / 2.4* per cent of the population. One of the best known *Māori / Aborigines* is *Cathy Freeman / Dame Kiri Te Kanawa.*

There are still many problems, but *National Sorry Day / the Waitangi Tribunal* has helped to make some things better for *Māori / the Aborigines.*

Now write one sentence of your own to add to each text.

4 Choose a city or part of Australia or New Zealand that you would like to visit. Find some more information about it, and make a poster or give a talk to your class. These websites can help you:

http://www.australia.com/
http://www.newzealand.com/travel

ABOUT THE AUTHOR

Christine Lindop was born in New Zealand and taught English in France and Spain before settling in Great Britain. She is the Series Editor for Bookworms Factfiles, and has written or co-written more than twenty books, including several Bookworms titles – *Sally's Phone* and *Red Roses* (Human Interest, Starter), *Ned Kelly: A True Story* (True Stories, Stage 1), and *Australia and New Zealand* (Factfiles, Stage 3). She has also adapted two volumes of short stories for Bookworms World Stories: *The Long White Cloud: Stories from New Zealand* (Stage 3) and *Doors to a Wider Place: Stories from Australia* (Stage 4). She has written for the Oxford Dominoes and Dolphin Readers series, and has worked on many other Oxford graded readers series, including Classic Tales, Hotshot Puzzles and Storylines.

She returns to New Zealand and Australia as often as she can, always forgetting what a long and expensive journey it is until it is too late. She has visited nine of the fourteen cities mentioned in this book, and still hopes to get to Hobart, Perth, Darwin, Brisbane, and Canberra one day. In her free time she likes reading, gardening, watching films, cooking, and making mosaics.

OXFORD BOOKWORMS LIBRARY

Classics • Crime & Mystery • Factfiles • Fantasy & Horror
Human Interest • Playscripts • Thriller & Adventure
True Stories • World Stories

The OXFORD BOOKWORMS LIBRARY provides enjoyable reading in English, with a wide range of classic and modern fiction, non-fiction, and plays. It includes original and adapted texts in seven carefully graded language stages, which take learners from beginner to advanced level. An overview is given on the next pages.

All Stage 1 titles are available as audio recordings, as well as over eighty other titles from Starter to Stage 6. All Starters and many titles at Stages 1 to 4 are specially recommended for younger learners. Every Bookworm is illustrated, and Starters and Factfiles have full-colour illustrations.

The OXFORD BOOKWORMS LIBRARY also offers extensive support. Each book contains an introduction to the story, notes about the author, a glossary, and activities. Additional resources include tests and worksheets, and answers for these and for the activities in the books. There is advice on running a class library, using audio recordings, and the many ways of using Oxford Bookworms in reading programmes. Resource materials are available on the website <www.oup.com/bookworms>.

The *Oxford Bookworms Collection* is a series for advanced learners. It consists of volumes of short stories by well-known authors, both classic and modern. Texts are not abridged or adapted in any way, but carefully selected to be accessible to the advanced student.

You can find details and a full list of titles in the *Oxford Bookworms Library Catalogue* and *Oxford English Language Teaching Catalogues*, and on the website <www.oup.com/bookworms>.

THE OXFORD BOOKWORMS LIBRARY
GRADING AND SAMPLE EXTRACTS

STARTER • 250 HEADWORDS

present simple – present continuous – imperative –
can/cannot, must – *going to* (future) – simple gerunds ...

Her phone is ringing – but where is it?

Sally gets out of bed and looks in her bag. No phone. She looks under the bed. No phone. Then she looks behind the door. There is her phone. Sally picks up her phone and answers it. *Sally's Phone*

STAGE 1 • 400 HEADWORDS

... past simple – coordination with *and*, *but*, *or* – subordination with *before*, *after*, *when*, *because*, *so* ...

I knew him in Persia. He was a famous builder and I worked with him there. For a time I was his friend, but not for long. When he came to Paris, I came after him – I wanted to watch him. He was a very clever, very dangerous man. *The Phantom of the Opera*

STAGE 2 • 700 HEADWORDS

... present perfect – *will* (future) – *(don't) have to, must not, could* – comparison of adjectives – simple *if* clauses – past continuous – tag questions – *ask/tell* + infinitive ...

While I was writing these words in my diary, I decided what to do. I must try to escape. I shall try to get down the wall outside. The window is high above the ground, but I have to try. I shall take some of the gold with me – if I escape, perhaps it will be helpful later. *Dracula*

STAGE 3 • 1000 HEADWORDS

… should, may – present perfect continuous – *used to* – past perfect
– causative – relative clauses – indirect statements …

Of course, it was most important that no one should see Colin, Mary, or Dickon entering the secret garden. So Colin gave orders to the gardeners that they must all keep away from that part of the garden in future. *The Secret Garden*

STAGE 4 • 1400 HEADWORDS

… past perfect continuous – passive (simple forms) –
would conditional clauses – indirect questions –
relatives with *where/when* – gerunds after prepositions/phrases …

I was glad. Now Hyde could not show his face to the world again. If he did, every honest man in London would be proud to report him to the police. *Dr Jekyll and Mr Hyde*

STAGE 5 • 1800 HEADWORDS

… future continuous – future perfect –
passive (modals, continuous forms) –
would have conditional clauses – modals + perfect infinitive …

If he had spoken Estella's name, I would have hit him. I was so angry with him, and so depressed about my future, that I could not eat the breakfast. Instead I went straight to the old house. *Great Expectations*

STAGE 6 • 2500 HEADWORDS

… passive (infinitives, gerunds) – advanced modal meanings –
clauses of concession, condition

When I stepped up to the piano, I was confident. It was as if I knew that the prodigy side of me really did exist. And when I started to play, I was so caught up in how lovely I looked that I didn't worry how I would sound. *The Joy Luck Club*

BOOKWORMS · FACTFILES · STAGE 3

The USA

ALISON BAXTER

Everybody knows about the United States. You can see its films, hear its music, and eat its food just about everywhere in the world. Cowboys, jazz, hamburgers, the Stars and Stripes – that's the United States.

But it's a country with many stories to tell. Stories of busy cities, and quiet, beautiful forests and parks. Stories of a country that fought against Britain, and then against itself, to make the United States of today. Stories of rich and poor, black and white, Native American and immigrant. And the story of what it is really like to be an American today . . .

BOOKWORMS · FACTFILES · STAGE 3

Information Technology

PAUL A. DAVIES

It is hard to imagine the modern world without information technology. At home, at work, and at play, mobile phones, e-mails and computers have become part of daily life.

The story of information technology is a story of machines – from the ancient abacus to the small powerful computer chips of today. But it is also a story of people. Meet a woman who wrote computer programs two hundred years ago, a teenage millionaire, a man who began with a paperclip and ended with a house – and the criminals who want your name and your money.

Come and discover the world of information technology.